BUILDING
BRAINPOWER

Firing Up Both Brains to Solve Problems and Get Faster Results

BUILDING BRAINPOWER

Firing Up Both Brains to Solve Problems and Get Faster Results

Copyright © 2011 by Elizabeth Ann Lawless

ISBN: 978-1-892324-05-4

Published by Adriel Publishing

Printed in the United States of America

www.Biz4Creatives.com

lizbiz4c@gmail.com

DEDICATION

For all of you life long learners who want to maintain a healthy brain and a creative outlook for more control and joy ... I salute you.

INTRODUCTION

As a creative marketing, advertising and promotion expert since 1988, I am continually amazed at how many people underestimate their ability to be creative and to use their brain to help them solve problems. It is one of the most powerful tools that we have and we don't access or apply it as much as we should.

Anyone can learn to use more of their brain. Brainpower helps you in all the areas of your life. **Building Brainpower: IS FUN!** If we want to continue to maintain a healthy brain, we must use it. The brain thrives on experience. If we want our brain to continue to grow, we must feed it as rich, as varied, and as stimulating an environment as possible.

STILL UNKNOWN

The brain is still a largely unknown frontier for medical scientists. The brain is very complex and mysterious, but every day new discoveries are made that explain a little more of the magic of the human mind. It is one of the greatest mysteries and we carry it with us all the time.

Although brain research has increased by leaps and bounds in the last 20 years there is always something new to learn. With new technology and funding scientist are finding out more and more. Many of the discoveries are expanding our education, clarifying brain activities and proving some previous thoughts false or only partially true.

However, this Book is not a scientific approach but one attempt to:
★ simplify some brain information

★ increase readers awareness of how the brain helps solve problems

★ offer steps to raise the level of creative and critical thinking of the reader

★ share ideas for becoming more creative

I believe learning about left and right brain characteristics, mastering creative and critical thinking and applying these thinking skills to our daily lives whether business, personal or social, helps us maintain a healthy brain, become whole-brain thinkers and achieve more success in business, relationships and life.

A SMALL FOUNDATION

The brain and how it works is fascinating. The Brain--the matter that makes up the mind--is 85 percent water. Out of the skull, it slumps like a blob of Jell-O.

Aristotle (384-322 B.C.) thought the brain's function was that of a radiator to cool the blood.

The brain does receive 20 percent of the body's blood supply, and he was partial correct, the brain can cool the blood solely through rational thought but that is only one small step.

Thomas Edison, although a great thinker, disliked exercise and believed the body's chief job was to carry around the brain.

Some people I am sure fall into the Edison belief category but most people never think about the brain at all.

Given it's compact size (about three pounds), efficient power consumption (similar to a 20-watt lightbulb) and massive storage capacity

(100 trillion bits of information), the brain is a compelling biological structure that can create magic, if we will learn to use and trust it.

FACTS ABOUT THE BRAIN

The brain lies wrapped in three cushioning layers of tissue or fibrous membranes within the protective walls of the skull. This amazing organ is more powerful and inventive than anything else on earth. It constantly fields waves of information about the world around it. Through the five (5) senses the brain gathers input then sorts, thinks, remembers, creates, compares, solves and coordinates life. It is even active while other body parts are at rest.

The brain consists of three main parts all of which do three distinctly different activities:

1. The cerebrum houses the cerebral hemispheres (left and right);
2. The cerebellum is concerned with coordination of movement; and
3. The brain stem unites the brain to the spinal cord which contains the intricate network of nerves connected to the rest of the body.

The front of the human brain, the cerebrum is larger and more developed than in all other animals. Scientists believe it to be the most complicated part of the whole brain. Past research has proven the left and right halves are better at different activities and newer research is proving a more multifaceted connection, but there is still much to discover.

The cortex or surface of the brain contains a complicated mass of 10 (ten) billion nerve cells, but this is only a tenth of the total cell count. The other ninety (90) billion cells make up the soft, jelly-like tissue. This thorough network of nerve fibers is connected to nerve cells all over the body. Millions of messages are carried on this network of pathways between the brain and the body every second of every day. The brain is the control center that talks to the rest of the body.

CEREBRUM

The Cerebrum is where thinking, learning, feeling and memories are stored, activated and engaged. Without the cerebrum, humans could not:

★ learn facts
★ write stories
★ love family and friends
★ work in business
★ and much, much more.

Individuals use these skills to pass on knowledge, build on what others have learned and create commerce, families and communities.

The neocortex is the section of the brain you usually see in pictures when someone is talking about the brain. The more folds and creases the neocortex has the more information it stores. A baby's brain is nearly as smooth as its bottom because it has not yet experienced learning.

"If all the nerves in your body were stretched out, they would be about seventy-five (75) miles!"

Jenny Bryan
Your Amazing Brain

A fully formed human brain contains 100 billion neurons or nerve cells. The number is not as important for intelligence as the connections between them. These connections begin to form in the last trimester before birth, growing rapidly until the age of about 10. With scientific confirmation of this growth pattern, it is evident now why a child can easily learn a new language in a foreign country, if he or she does so at the age when the brain cells that process language are being wired.

CEREBELLUM

Cerebellum — The cerebellum connected to the brain stem is primarily concerned with coordination of movements. It integrates the information coming from all the senses with all the muscles so as to produce smooth, finely tuned movements. Without the cerebellum, humans could not:

★ sit

★ walk

★ dance to iTunes or others

★ work in the yard

★ paint pictures

★ play musical instruments

★ participate in sports

★ and much, much more.

BRAIN STEM

Brain Stem –- The brain stem is situated on top of the spinal cord it contains a very intricate network of nerves about the size of a little finger called the reticular formation. It receives nerves from all areas of the brain and likewise sends out nerves in every direction maintaining wakefulness. It also monitors and filters information coming in through the senses.

By the time humans are six years old their brains have reached 90% of their total size. Genes alone don't determine how a child's brain develops. The environment – nutrition, care and stimulation – significantly affects the brain.

Further brain growth results from increasing the number of connectors between neurons through learning experiences. Connections within the brain develop at different times, providing windows of opportunity for specific types of learning.

Since the brain mass increases but skull size is static, folds develop in the brain's surface and the entire surface becomes more enfolded as you experience and learn new things. The brain continues growing until about the early twenties, but connections continue as long as we continue to learn or experience new things. The brain functions as a whole, integrating emotional, social, cognitive and physical aspects of development.

Chemists, biologists, physicists, psychologists, and mathematicians still cannot come up with a formula for the operations that go on regularly inside each person's head. Scientists are continually learning about how the brain works, but many questions remain. However, a major question has been answered, the brain holds the key to who and what we are.

> *"Who you are speaks so loudly,*
> *I cannot hear what you say!"*
> *Ralph Waldo Emerson*

This has always been the most important question that each of us asks ourselves. Who Am I? We won't find all of the answers with this text today, but we can learn some important things about ourselves and others. We can also learn some tips for living more successfully and living in harmony with others.

BRAIN DOMINANCE PATTERNS

All humans learn in different ways: visually (sight), orally (sound) or kinesthetically (movement) and have different behavior and temperaments (sanguine/talker; phlegmatic/watcher; choleric/worker; melancholic/thinker).

In addition to temperament and learning styles, I believe most of us have a brain dominance preference.   What I mean is we approach problems in our life from a particular side of the brain (our preference) most of the time. If that is true, then with awareness, discovery and practice we can continue **building more brainpower.**

Hemisphericity Theory is the study of left and right brain characteristics and although scientist don't hold to this theory much any more because they believe the brain applies a more whole brain or multilayered approach, I think that we can take knowledge about left and right brain characteristics and use it to enhance our lives whether in business, at home or in society.

It is my conviction that most people have a brain dominance pattern, either left or right. This means that when faced with problems they tend to take a certain approach (left critical or right creative) when dealing with the particular situation. **There is no right or wrong brain dominance pattern.** Most people just have a preference or tendency to go through life using a particular side of the brain to deal with school, work, friends, family and situations.

We have all heard that humans only use 10% of their brain's potential. It might be more now as we continue to learn more about how the brain operates. But if this is true then you can **increase your brainpower** by learning about the different hemispheres of the brain and how they work, separately and together. Most of the time individuals work out of a dominant side of the brain.

As we look at left and right brain characteristics, a particular brain dominance preference should become clear in the reader's mind, if you don't already know which direction you lean.

The reason for studying about the brain and how it works, is individuals begin to understand that they (and the people in their lives) do something for a reason, because they have a particular brain preference. Not because they are slow or smart, or because they want to irritate another person. They just process information and make decisions in a different way than the person next to them.

A FEW EXAMPLES

Are you the type of person that needs things neat and orderly? Do you like to have a schedule and keep to it? Or do you live in chaos, juggling several activities or projects at once and time falls low on your list of things to think about?

When you were a kid did you make a floor plan for that fort and did you take the same route every day to your friend's house? Or did you grab some pieces of wood and started nailing them together, or maybe find a big cardboard box to play in and then convince your friends to go exploring the neighborhood?

When you cook do you follow the recipe exactly or do you throw in extra stuff to make your own creation?

Are you beginning to get a feel for your brain preference? **Remember there is no right or wrong here only the first response and your personal preference.** It doesn't mean that you don't occasionally lean the other way or persuade someone to do it your way. We are just trying to become more aware and practice both approaches so that we can strengthen our whole brain approach to thinking and problem solving.

Each hemisphere is responsible for specific tasks that keep humans living, while other activities are shared by both sides.

It is a well known fact that most people process **numbers** in the **left side** of the brain and **letters** in the **right side** of the brain. However, in the brains of postal workers in Canada, which has zip codes that combine letters and numbers, the two areas of cognition are *closer* *together* than citizens from other countries that only use numbers. As you continue to read, you will see that the brain has the amazing ability to adapt, change or reformat itself.

The right and left brain can work on the same problem, but will use opposite processes. When the two sides work together or interact (switch back and forth) properly you have whole brain thinking.

A person who wants to learn, grow or stretch their mental agility will study the brain and how it works, will learn to recognize left and right brain skills and seek to continue **building more brainpower.** By recognizing our own thinking styles and the thinking styles of others, we can alter and adapt as necessary.

It's not that one side of the brain is better than the other, it's that **both sides are important.**

We need to learn how to shift consciously from one brain-style to another to meet the demands of living and working in a complex world. Everyone has two distinct thinking processes regardless of whether they have a left, right or double dominance tendency.

Critical and creative thinking exists in the cerebral hemisphere and when you have a thought the cerebral cortex telegraphs the information or impulse from the brain stem through the network of nerve fibers to nerve cells throughout the body. This amazing network of pathways continuously carries millions of messages from the brain to all the parts of your body.

WE RARELY THINK ABOUT IT

The brain works so efficiently, humans are hardly conscious of the exchange. For instance, the brain automatically says to the body, *hand pick up that piece of paper on the floor. Or feet avoid that desk when exiting the office.* Most humans don't have to think about breathing, blinking, sleeping, food digestion, sitting or walking. Your body and brain does it automatically.

The brain is the captain or chief of the body. Communication is the main function of the central nervous system. Within individual nerve cells, or neurons, signals are predominately electrical. Signals that are transmitted from one neuron to another are chemical. Challenging the brain to keep it in optimal condition is vital not only to the central nervous system, but also to the entire body. That's why it is important to learn new things.

The analytical and verbal skills are housed in the left hemisphere of the brain. The intuitive and visual are seated in the right. There is a connector, the corpus callosum, through which the two halves communicate.

As business people, heads of households or contributors to the community, we must have an open mind when it comes to studying the brain and exercising it to keep it strong. We must put away our preconceived notions, negative thoughts and sometimes even previous learning to explore and discover new thoughts.

Many adults believe they are not creative and consider creative activities out of their reach, that mystical, unattainable something that others have the talent for, but not them. In fact this is not the case, everyone has a brain and it can be fired up to meet the challenges of life.

With knowledge and practice any individual can become a more critical and creative thinker, thereby strengthen the whole brain and making better and faster decisions.

(For a list of *Great Books About the Brain* email: lizbiz4c@gmail.com).

LEFT AND RIGHT BRAIN CHARACTERISTICS

It is interesting to remind ourselves or explore the left and right sides of the brain and the particular characteristics of each. Many of you may know this information but it doesn't hurt to review things. Take a minute to print these pages or if you can't access a printer just write the characteristics down on a piece of paper then put a check mark by the ones that best describe you:

LEFT HEMISPHERE

Facts First

Logical

Let's Plan It

Linear

Sequential

Worker

Knowledge

Language

Math

Law

Rules

Symbols

Fact-oriented

Implement

Think words & figures

Serious

RIGHT HEMISPHERE

Feelings First

Chaotic

Lets Do It

Holistic

Spontaneous

Playful

Imagination

Art

Music

Dance

Intuition

Spatial

People-oriented

Creative

Think in pictures

Dreamer

We need both sides of the brain. They work together. For instance the left side recognizes the words or sentences and the right side recognizes the metaphor or tone (sarcasm), but both sides address language. The right side seems most concerned with new images or connections while the left side is essential for evaluating and shaping the connections.

Some props might be needed for this section. One way to understand the two sides of the brain is to image one gray sock and one white sock. By placing the white sock on the right hand and the gray sock on the left hand, making fists and bringing them together with the thumbs toward the body. You can create a pretty good example of the brain.

GRAY SOCK

Imagine looking at the hand with the gray sock (left hand). If you are from the boomer generation, a well-known phase during our parent and grandparents day was, *"He has a lot of gray matter."* Most sayings that are passed down for years are based in some truth and this is no exception. If you cut the brain open that's what you will see. The left side of the brain resembles gray matter due to the concentration of blood vessels and lack of myelin. Gray matter or stuff that sometimes is considered smart by society's standards includes: facts, figures, dates, schedules, logic, reason and other left brain activities discussed in this Book.

Let's consider another example, does this sound familiar? *"You need to drop off some clothes at the cleaner. You leave the house 10-15 minutes early for work. You decide before you leave the house which cleaners you want to use. You choose one on the right side of the road so you don't have to cross traffic and possibly wait on any oncoming cars. You go to the cleaners, drop the clothes and are back on the road with plenty of time to make it to work."* If this sounds familiar, you might be a **left brain dominant individual**.

The left side of the brain is determined to keep life sensible, organized and on schedule. Left Brain Dominant people arrive on time, take the shortest route and many times can calculate numbers in their head or memorize details quicker. Since it speaks, reads and computes for us, the left brain is a vital part of our daily life.

WHITE SOCK

Now imagine looking at the hand with the white sock (right hand). The right side of the brain is host to motor skills, intuition, and emotion and it is a ready receptor of music and sound. As a problem-solver, the right brain looks at the whole situation, and often the solution materializes as if by magic.

The reason we used a white sock on the right hand is because the right side of the brain is white. Cells are coated with an insulating substance called myelin. Myelination reduces interference noise, allowing nerve cells to process signals more clearly and transmit them more quickly. Myelination in humans occurs with need; the areas of the brain that are most concerned with survival myelinate first. Thus the right side of the brain is whiter than the left, since it houses the essential intuitive, feeling, and reactive skills.

White matter skills are especially valuable in emergency or survival situations, when a driver swerves into our lane on the highway, a strange dog barks at us or a tornado is spotted nearby.

If during the previous cleaners example you were saying to yourself *I don't even know which cleaners I left my clothes at, much less what side of the road it's on* then I have good news and bad news. The good news is there is a viable reason you can't remember, you're predominantly a right brain person and it's not on the top of your radar. The bad news is I might not be able to help you find that group of clothes, but by practicing a left brain approach you can keep from loosing any more.

Let's look at some other examples. Does this sound familiar? *How many of you have your watch set ahead of time? Go ahead tell the truth you are the only one here, you can admit it. How about this when you give directions do you say go until you see the Wendy's turn right and go down to the Church and take a left? On Friday afternoon do you say "Let's take a trip to Austin, get packed and get in the car and go?* If this sounds like you then you lean toward a **right brain dominance pattern**.

Everyone accesses both sides of their brain as they go through the day. It's just that most people have a strong tendency to lean one way or the other -- either left or right when faced with a problem or situation.

Once you understand which is your strong side or initial approach, then you can begin to do exercises that will train your less dominant side. That way when you need to call on a particular part of your brain for a solution to a problem or situation, you can take a left and right, or more importantly a whole brain approach.

I think humans are born with these left and right brain dominance tendencies, but some individuals are heavily influenced by family and society. For instance an accountant who likes to garden or a fireman who loves history.

Many people work at a job or get training to follow in a parent or grandparents footsteps because it is a tradition in the family and not because it is what they love. Others take a job because of what it pays or because they think they can make a better living and then find out that they really don't like the day to day activities that it takes to do the job. It is possible to develop the less preferred side.

(For some exercises to enhance left or right brain thinking, email lizbiz4c@gmail.com **and I will email you back some exercise sheets.)**

There are also a lot of people who are married to or work with people who have a different brain dominant pattern, personality or learning preference. What you find when you study these issues is that people do things for a reason because that is how they are wired or programmed internally. If you understand why a person reacts or behaves in a certain way, it frees you to accept and appreciate their differences. You can agree to disagree about something while maintaining the relationship whether business or personal.

Boosting brainpower can be accomplished by expanding our awareness, learning new things, and by developing and applying more of the brain's capacity. Working crossword or other puzzles, learning new words every day, studying another language or engaging in a new hobby that has it's own special language and skills, all enhance mental strength and improve mental agility which holds off some brain related diseases.

Learning how the brain works and which brain dominance preference (left or right) is preferred, can be key to developing a balanced lifestyle. It also helps us reinforce positive thoughts, helps us resist negative internal and external assaults and helps us relate better to others. Having a certain base of knowledge and understanding also helps to pinpoint breakdowns in ourselves and others and enables us to find faster solutions to problems.

CRITICAL THINKING

Developing methods that extend critical thinking in work, home or social situations can have tremendous benefits and with today's global and competitive environment it is crucial. Critical comes from the word critic -- skilled in judgement.   Critical (adjective) means of decisive importance with respect to outcome; to determine or decide.

Critical thinking involves the ability to raise powerful questions about what is being read, listened to or viewed.   Thinking also involves developing the ability to assess information and make creative and critical judgments.   This is especially important today with the Internet and access to so much information, good, bad, mediocre or great. We cant take things at face or rather screen value, we must consider the reliability of the source.

Take a few minutes now and think about this question then write down a few names and why you thought of this person. It might be a famous person, a member of your family, a friend or co-worker.

Do you know someone who is a Critical Thinker?

Depending on the field of study, the area of commerce or our brain dominance pattern we can spend less time than we should applying one of the thinking styles either critical or creative. One of the thinking approaches gets brushed aside in favor of the thinking skills that we access more readily.

People in left brain professions may be less likely to apply creative thinking while people in right brain professions may pass on applying critical thinking to a situation. Success comes from combining detail and logic with a sense of overview and invention.

The tendency to make judgements about individuals who respond in a particular way (maybe different from our own) is sometimes challenging. That is why intelligence must be viewed from different sides as well as different ways.

"Standardized tests have systematically ignored the wide range of abilities that are valued within our culture, and they are of

little use in helping us to recognize and educate individuals of eminence."

Bruce Torff
Multiple Intelligences and Assessment

Reasoning programs that treat thinking in a generic way, indifferent to new media and the demands of different tasks, are taking intelligence out of context.

CREATIVE THINKING

Creative thinking comes from create a verb which means to cause to exist, to give rise to; bring about; into being; originate; produce. Creative (adjective) means having the ability or power to create things; creating; productive; characterized by originality; imagination. Creativity is the noun and creatively the adverb.

We can't cause something to exist without taking action. Since almost every individual has a will or the ability to take action, every individual also has the capacity to create. Just because someone creates with facts and figures instead of paints or harmony does not make it any less a part of the creative process.

Definitions are not enough, but they give us the real flavor and feeling of the words we use. Words grow and change like living things and carry their existence with them.

Now take a few minutes and think about this question then write down a few names and why you thought of this person. Again, it might be a famous person, a member of your family, a friend or co-worker.

Do you know someone who is a Creative Thinker?

Humans are made up of three faculties: thinking, feeling and acting. Each of us performs these activities unconsciously. We hear a lot about thinking and feeling from science to psychology, but we hear less about the will—taking action.

The goal with this text, is to discover new ideas, new patterns of thinking and new ways to make our lives more successful or harmonious, **and then to act.**

(To learn more about creative thinking or to engage in a series of creative exercises visit Amazon **and purchase my book** *Creative Monster* **or email** lizb4c@gmail.com **to**

purchase my *Creative Monster Kit* which includes seven days of activities. Great for kids or adults who want to explore their creative side.)

Creative thinking is important because forces around us demand action. If we have problems, we must seek solutions. Creativity or creative thinking is available to each of us. Creative thinking opens the door to more than one solution for any problem.

Creative thinking is important because:

★ It keeps our mind active.

★ Complex problems need creative solutions.

★ It helps us develop new ways to do things.

★ Changes in technology occur almost daily.

★ Social customs demand it.

★ It improves our individual and collective life.

Sometimes that will mean embracing change and that's not always easy.

> *"The reasonable woman/man adapts herself /himself to the world. The unreasonable woman/man attempts to adapt the world to herself/himself. Therefore all progress depends on the unreasonable woman/man."*
>
> George Bernard Shaw
> (modified by Liz Lawless)

We will increasingly be called on to evaluate technology or resources while working with different personalities and agendas. Whether it is adjusting to different business opportunities, working with different cultures, learning new technology, providing new services, or changing job assignments, we must learn to cope quickly.

Yesterday's solutions may not solve the problems of today because they are guaranteed to be obsolete tomorrow. New information changes circumstances. New people entering the situation can change the approach and the outcome. Change forces us to make choices.

We can complain that things are not as easy as they used to be, or we can use our critical and creative thinking abilities to find new possibilities, new solutions and new ideas. We need to trust our brain more, to enhance our decision-making skills and increase our mental strength with the new realities we face each day. We need to keep **building more brainpower!**

And once we have made progress ourselves, then the goal might be to instill these approaches in our children so they can build self-confidence, trust in their decision-making skills, and develop the mental strength to deal with this new society regardless of what the future holds.

"Critical and creative thinking are life resources for problem-solving, inventing, designing and decision-making."

Elizabeth Ann Lawless

The more we learn, the more we realize that people don't purposely do things to irritate us, they just think or learn differently than we do.

The most important thing about the brain is it not only works in a linear step-by-step fashion, but also performs parallel processing, integrating and synthesizing information that it sees, hears, smells, touches and tastes, and abstracting from it generalities.

For instance, the human brain has the astonishing ability to recognize in about a second:

★ a face

★ a song

★ a mother's perfume

★ a favorite food

★ a texture

and a thousand other activities.

The brain constantly deals with floods of information about the world around us--from our eyes, ears, nose, mouth and extremities. Our brain sorts, thinks, remembers, creates, compares, solves and coordinates. Even when we sleep it is still active, generating ideas to zap us with the next morning. The ideal person has strong skills in each hemisphere (left and right) of the brain and can move back and forth when those skills are needed.

The more we make whole-brained decisions, the more balanced we will have in our lives. Whole-brain thinking helps us make good choices, deal with changes in our life and eases worry about the unknown, because we know we have the ability to critically and creatively find solutions to cope with any situation.

Left and right brain thinking can be crucial to successful and harmonious living. Make every day life a brain gym where you are your own personal trainer. What you think becomes the actions you take.

Take the right steps and keep building brainpower! You can do this and it is easier than you think.

Just start a daily practice of One Creative Action.

For ideas be sure to visit my social media pages or website below or tune into my weekly Creative Passions Results podcast at www.anchor.fm/biz4creatives.

Please let me know if you have any breakthroughs. You can contact me by email: lizbiz4c@gmail.com or follow me at www.facebook.com/biz4creatives or online at www.Biz4Creatives.com.

Cheers to your success and to all of us become more whole brain thinkers.

Elizabeth Ann Lawless
Creative • Author • Speaker • Podcast Host

Liz is a Biz4Creatives Activist. She spends her day in Creative Action along with assisting others who desire to pursue their highest Creative Life in pursuit of their publishing, purpose, professional or performing passions.

She can be found on most social media, book publishing and podcast platforms or you can always visit her website for news, masterminds, retreats or appearances at:

www.Biz4Creatives.com

To listen to her podcast:

Creative Passions Results
visit
www.anchor.fm/biz4creatives

or check out her other books:

CREATIVES: It's A Biz Lifestyle
A 7 Step Guide To Profiting From Your
Creative Passion

Your Best-Seller Book: 5 Steps To Quicker
Publishing Success

How To Study The Bible: A Jump Start for New
Christians or Believers Who Never Studied Much

Western Legends: Yesterday & Today...African
Americans 1798 to 2009

Firing Up Both Brains: Teaching Youth Left &
Right Brain Thinking ... A Guide for Middle
School Librarians & Teachers

Creative Monster / Monstro Creativo

www.ingramcontent.com/pod-product-compliance
Lightning Source LLC
Chambersburg PA
CBHW071348200326
41520CB00013B/3155